Colorful Cities

Colorful Cities

Fun and Fanciful Buildings and Urban Designs

By
Alisa Calder

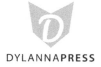

DYLANNAPRESS

The *Colorful Cities: Fun and Fanciful Buildings and Urban Designs* contains 36 creative city designs for a fun and relaxing way to unwind and relieve stress. Each full-page illustration contains intricate and creative designs, ranging from simple to complex, that together will provide hours of stress-free entertainment. The Coloring Pages for Grown-Ups series is designed for adults, teens, older children, and artists of all ages.

Coloring books for adults are considered a form of art therapy. It has been shown that coloring is a great way to relieve stress, calm the mind, and even reduce anxiety.

Coloring can also boost creativity by stimulating areas within the brain and helping to release endorphins. Many people consider coloring to be a form of meditation.

So grab your coloring pencils, crayons, or watercolors and start coloring!

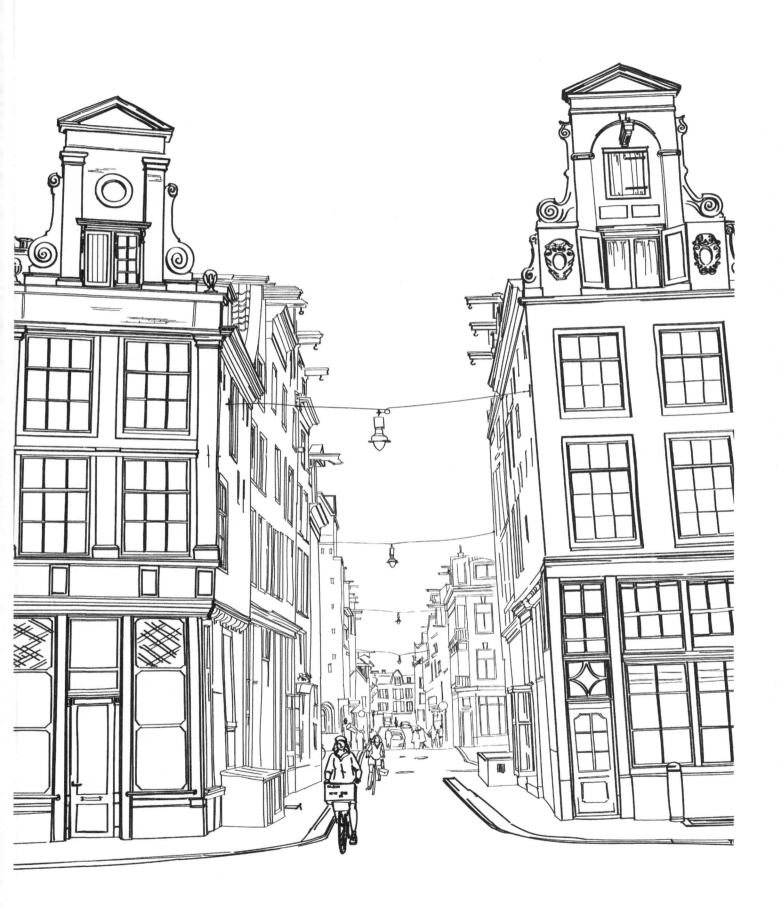

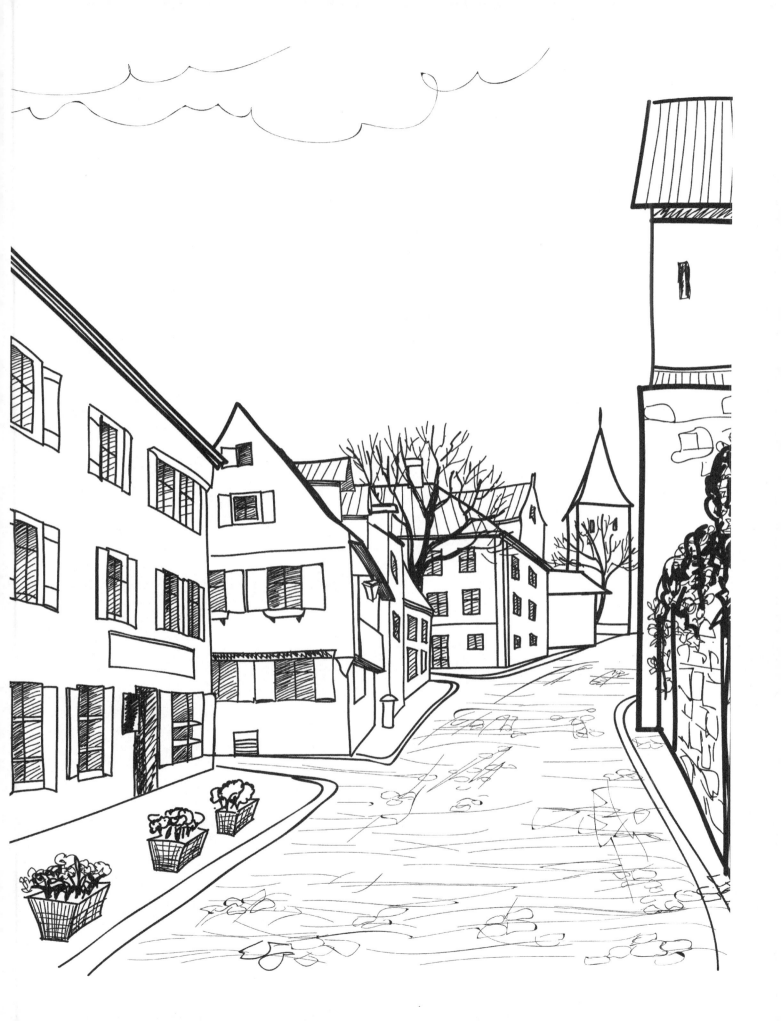

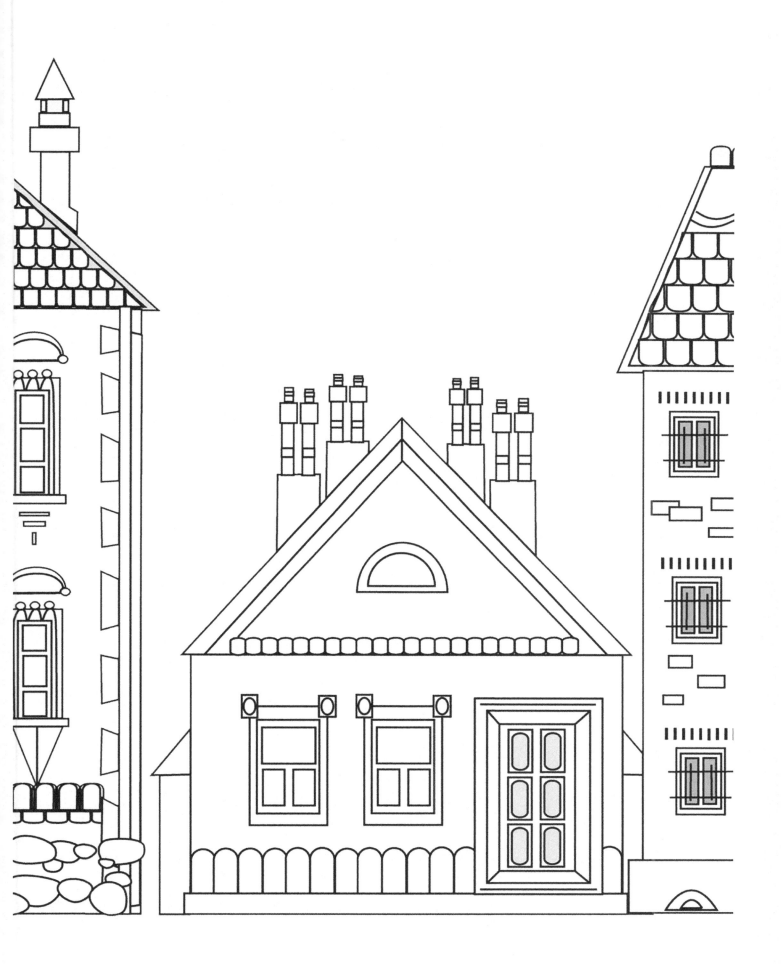

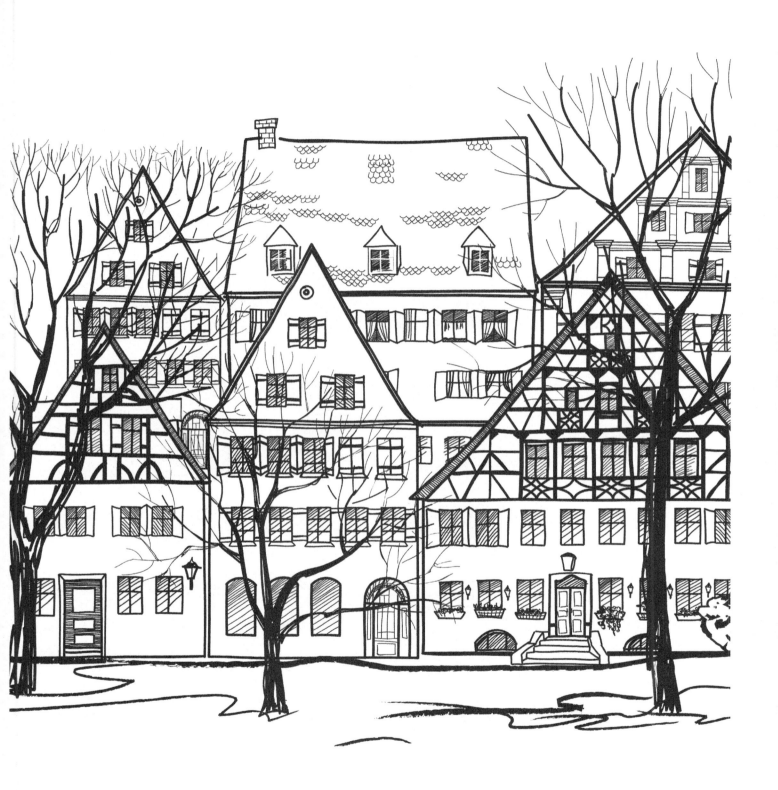

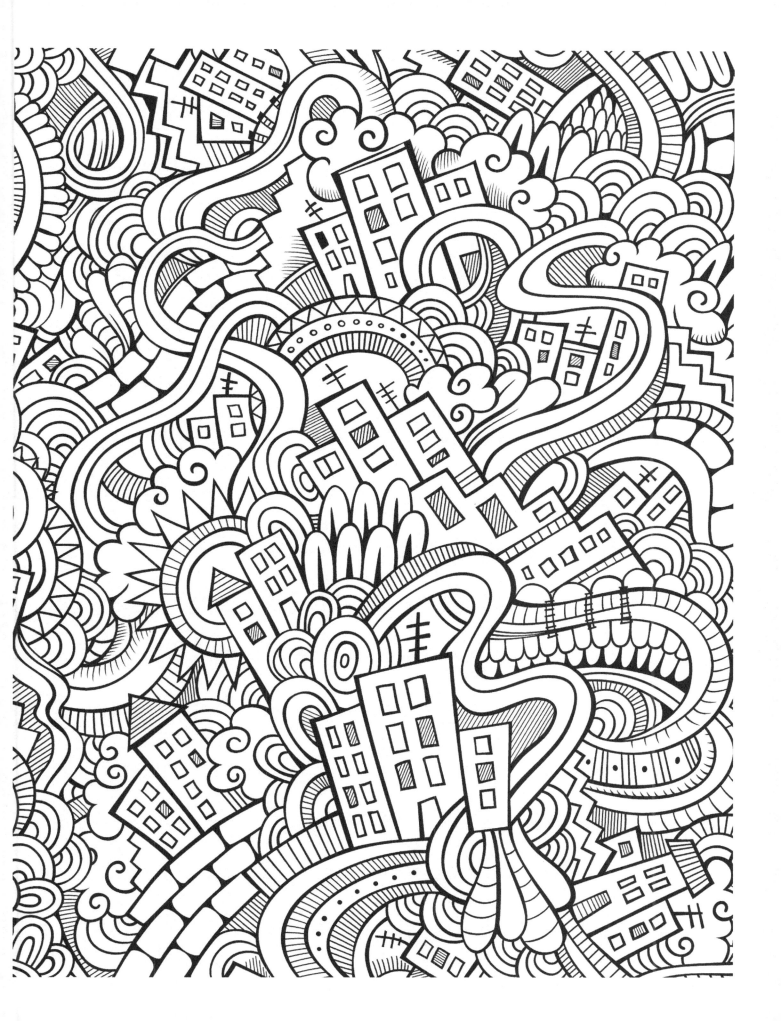

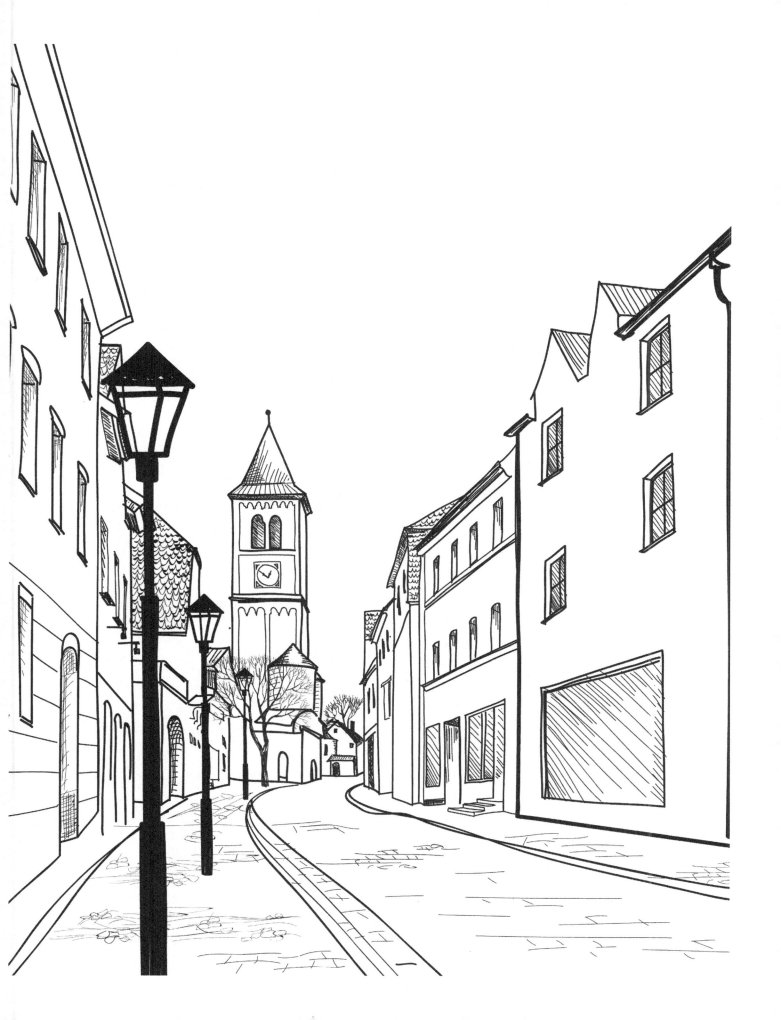

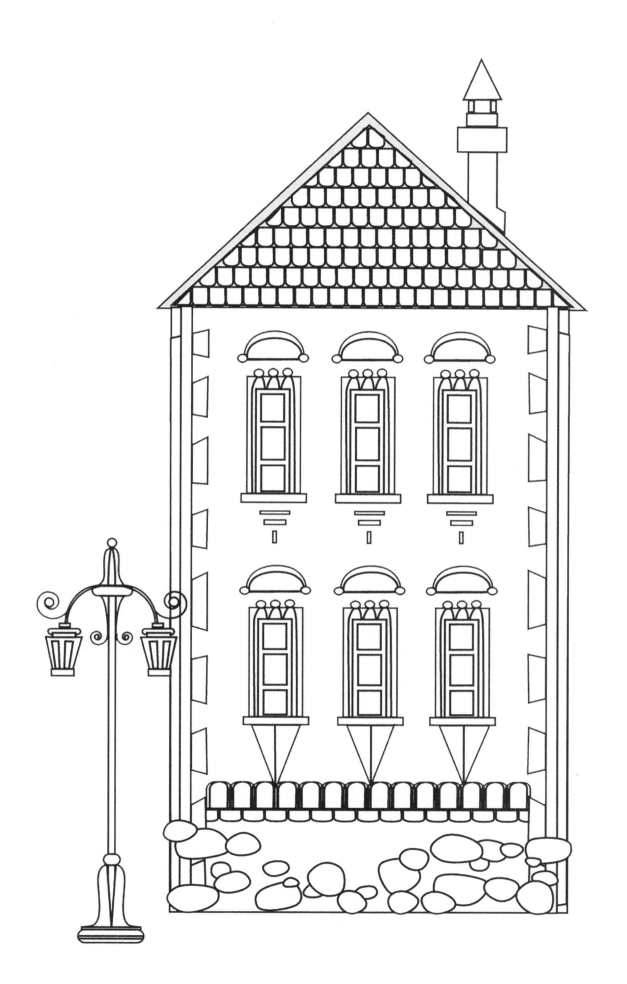

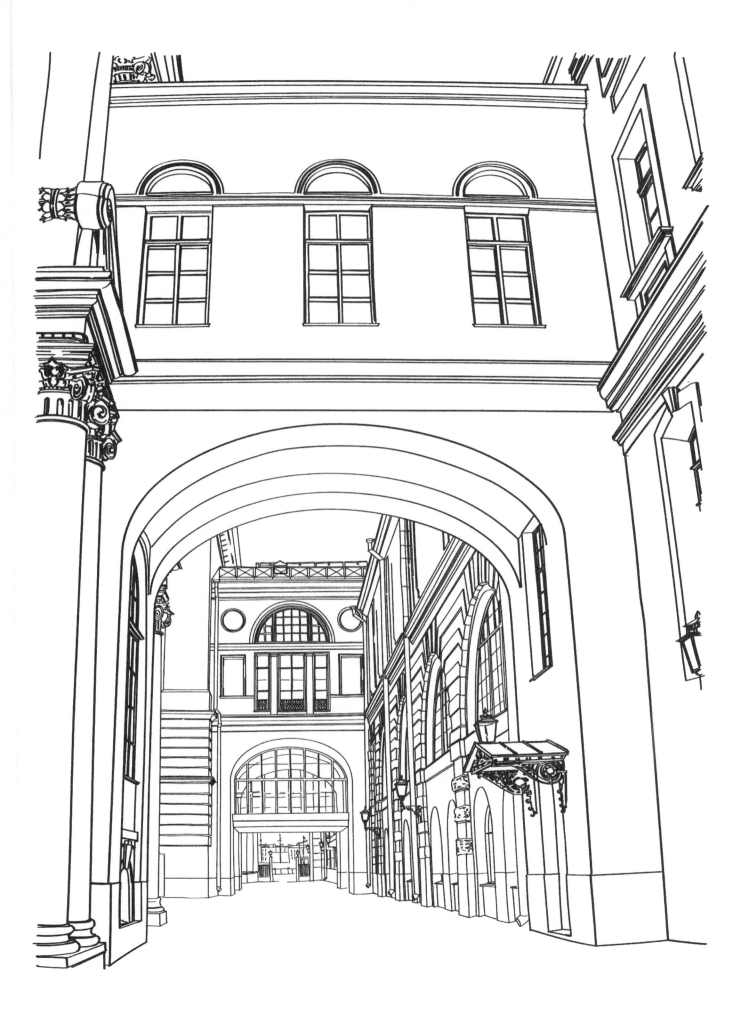

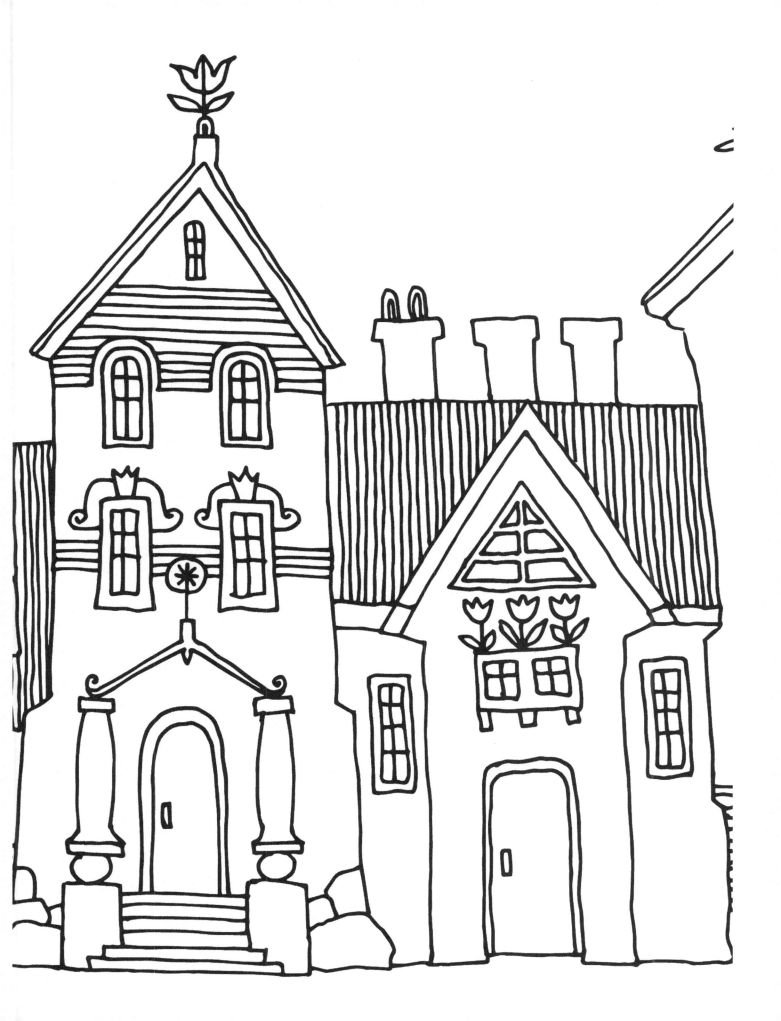

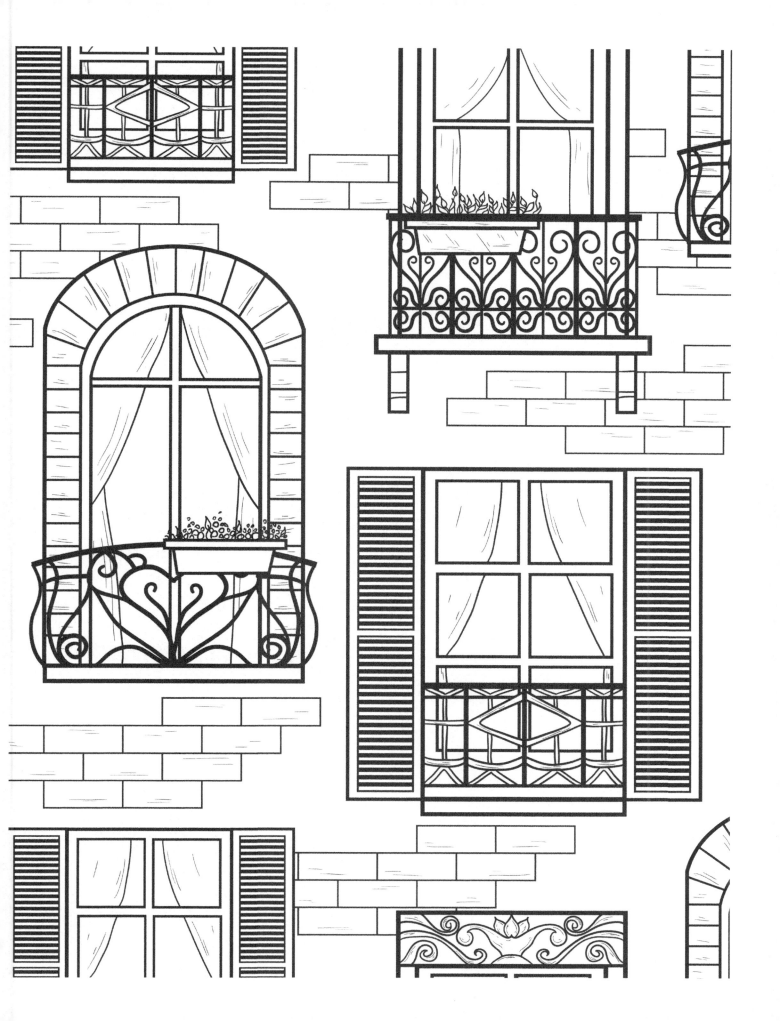

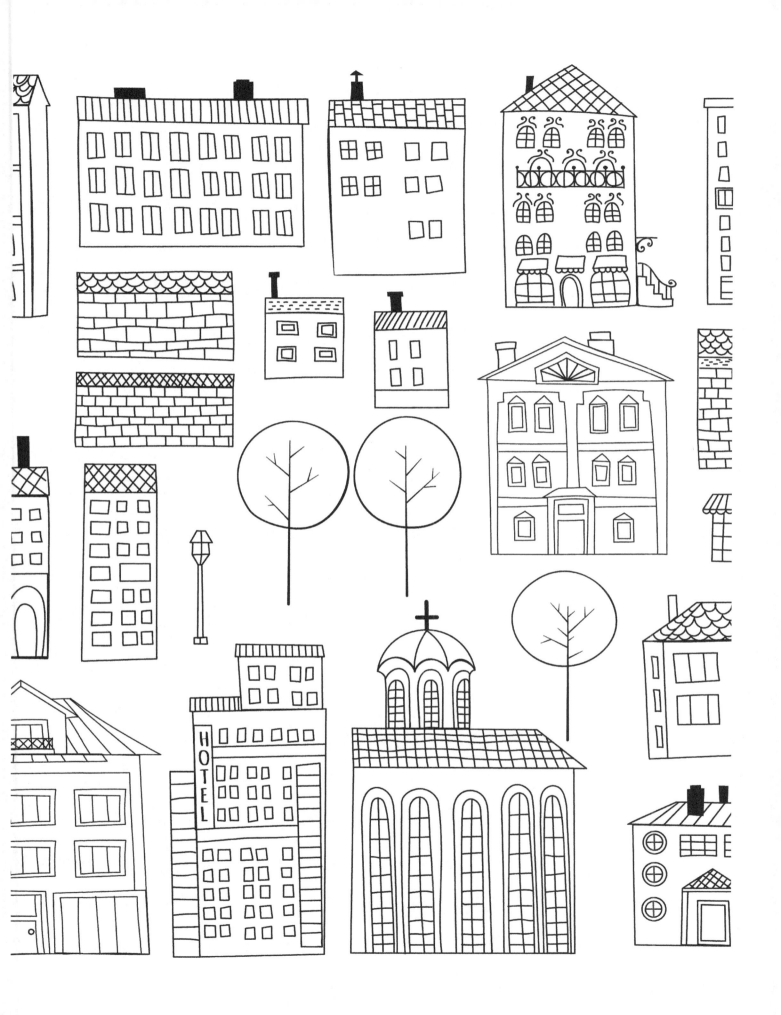

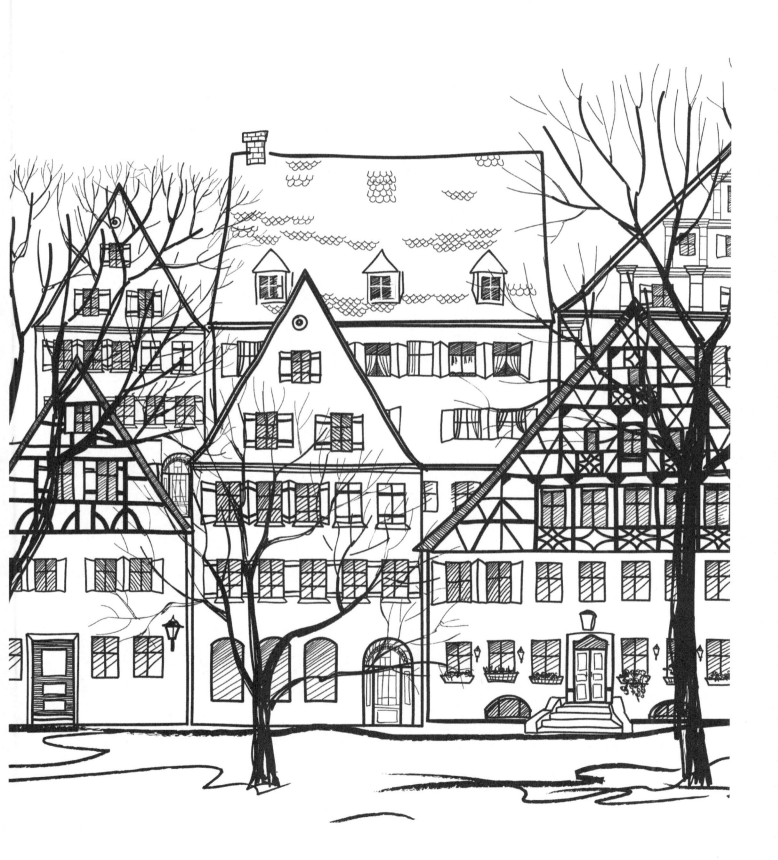

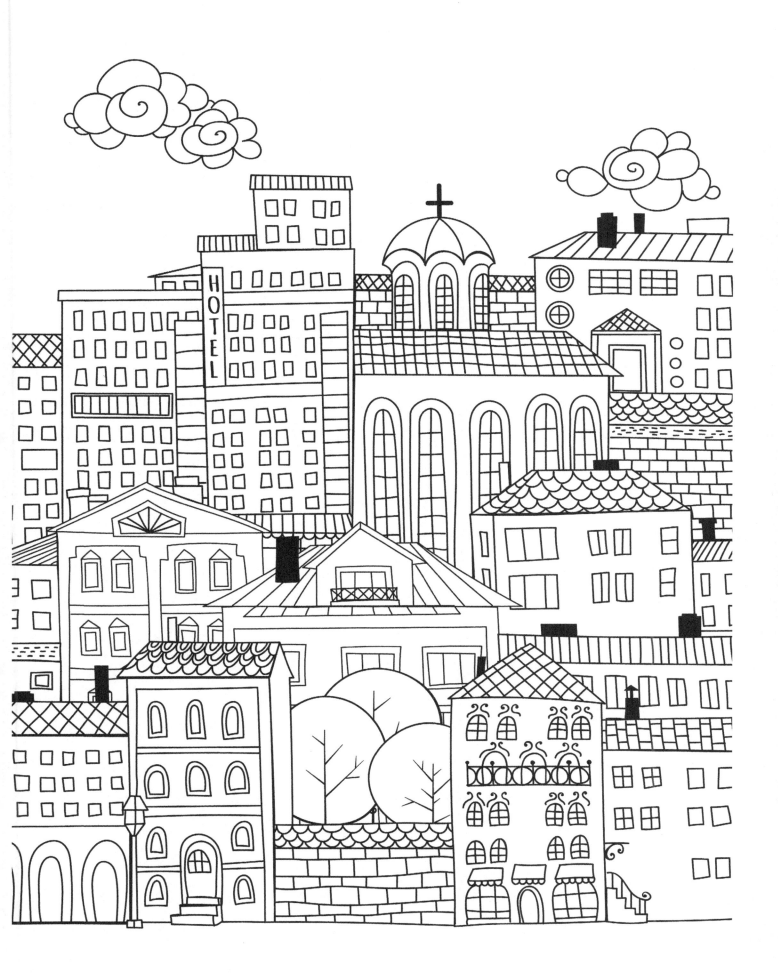

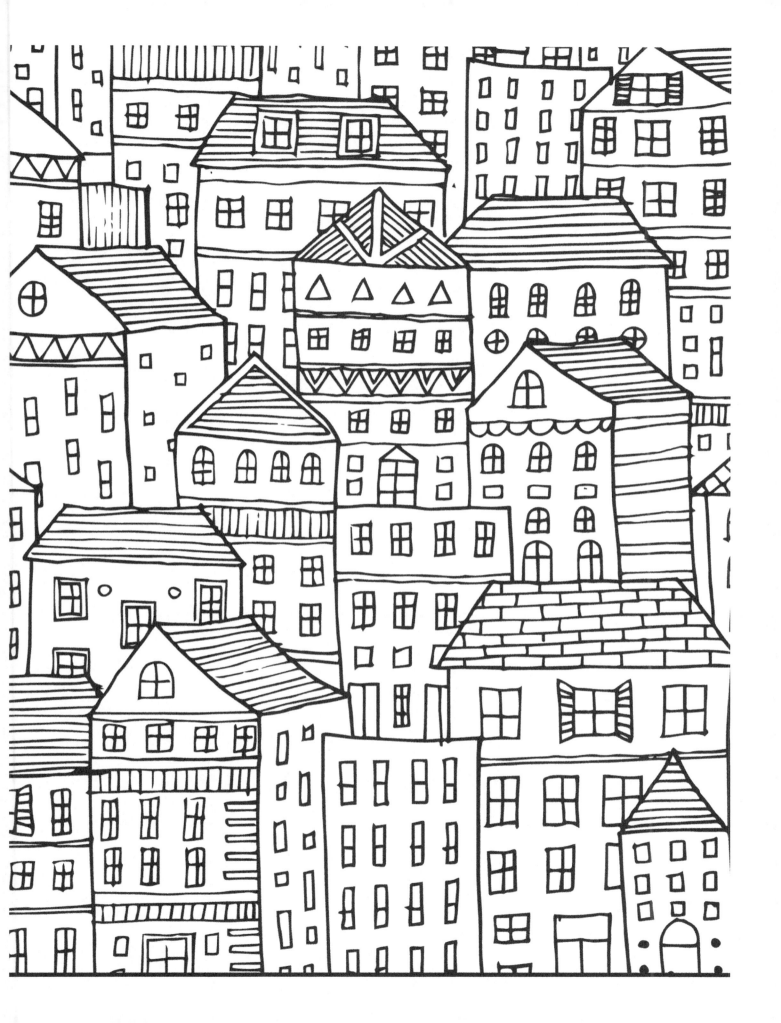

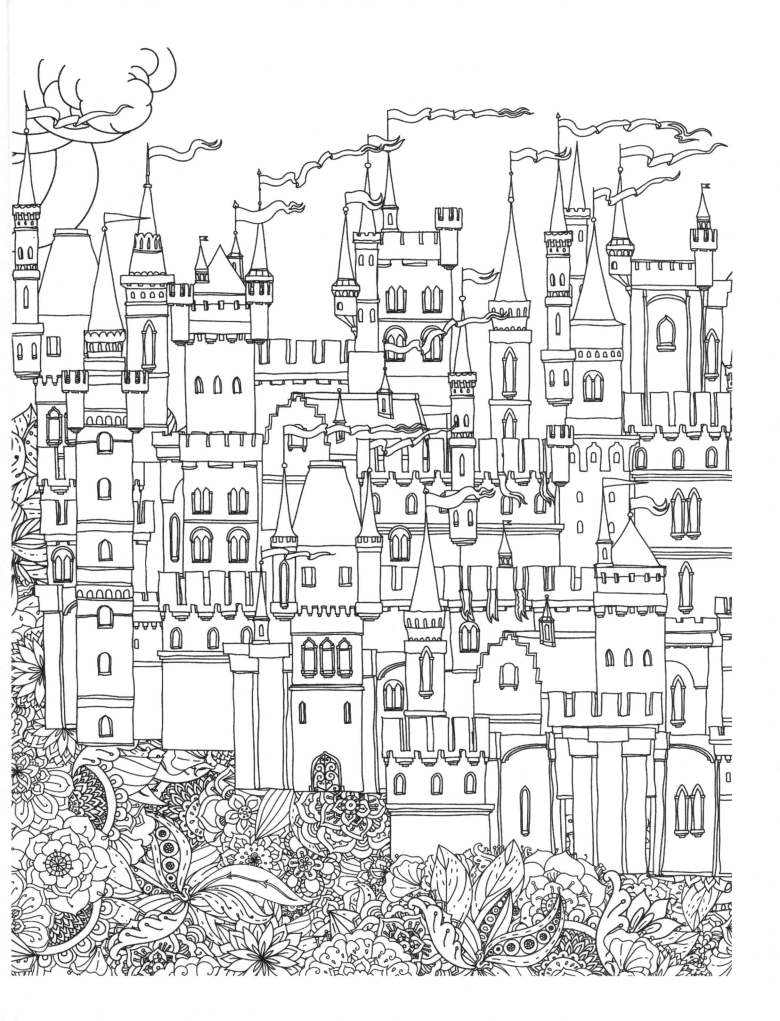

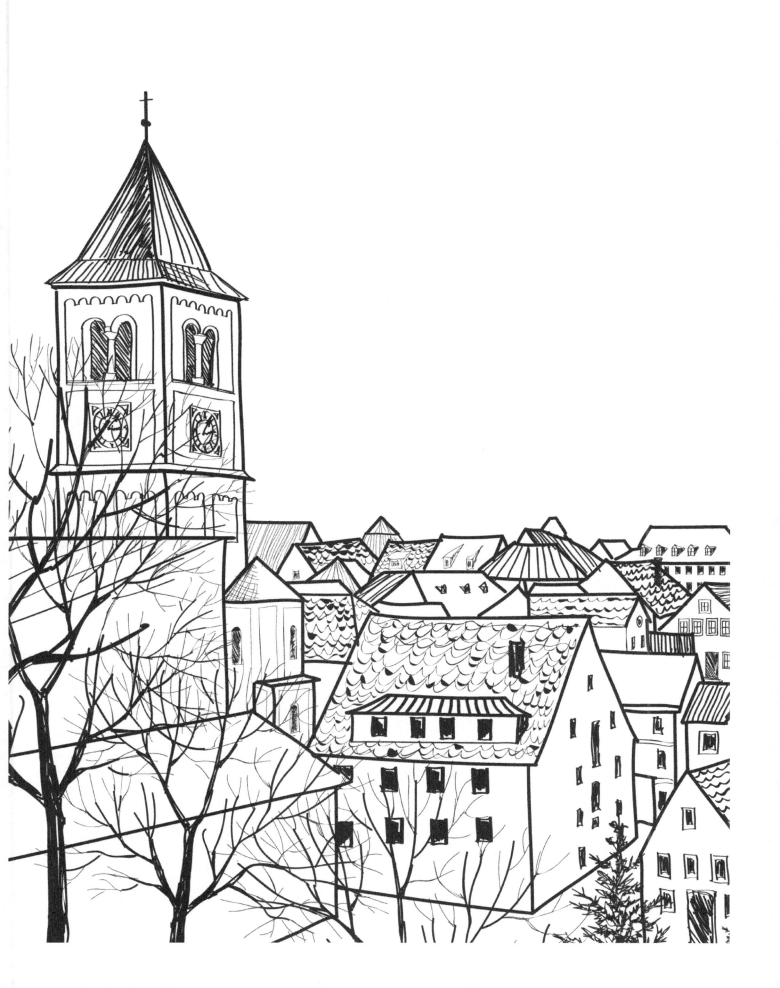

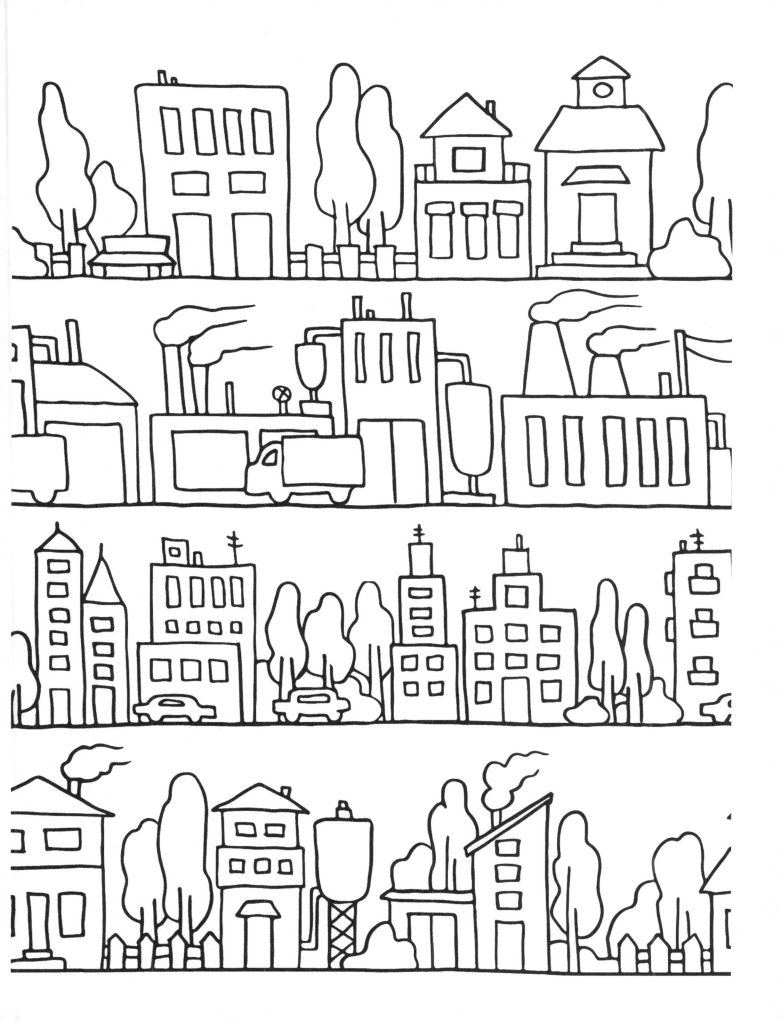

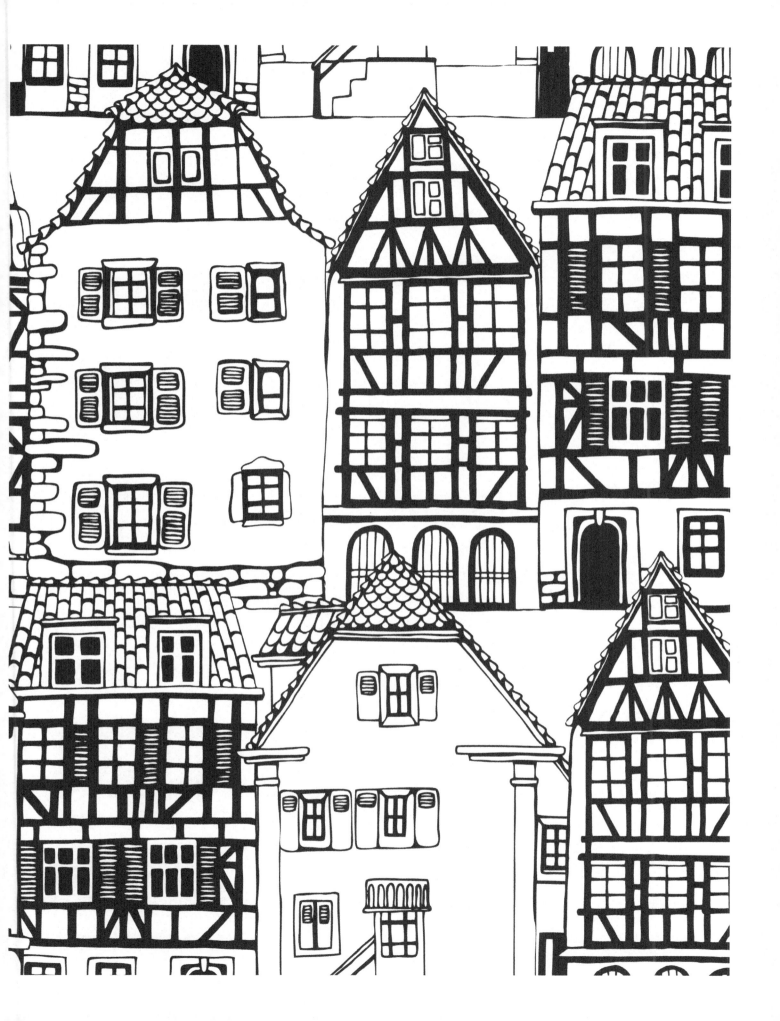

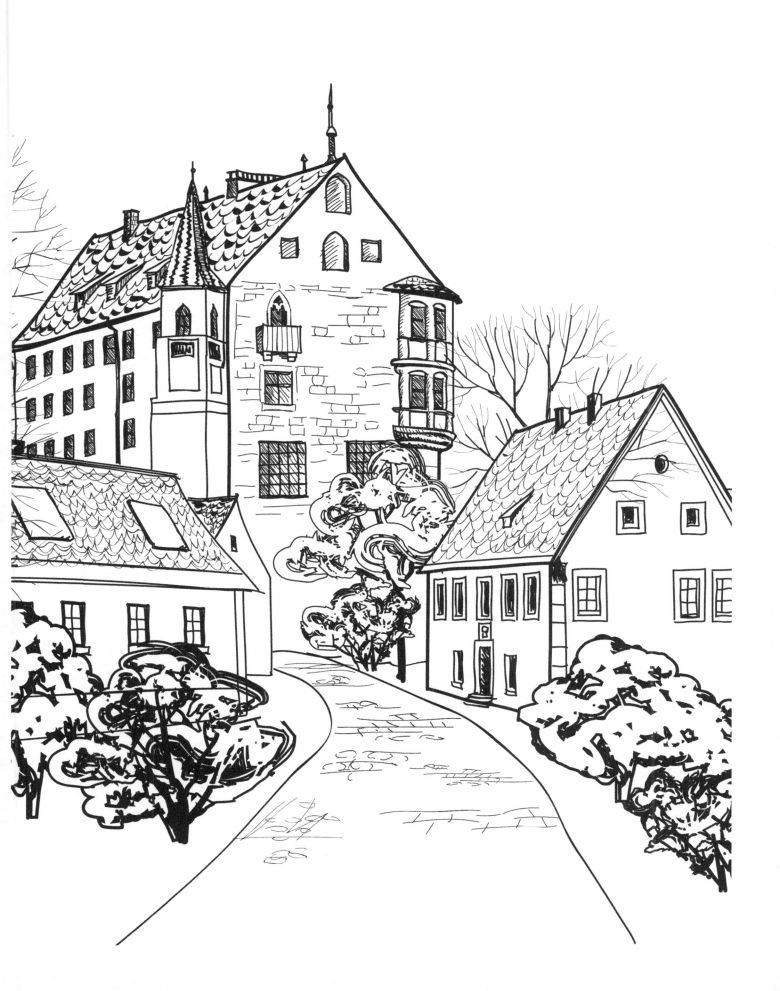

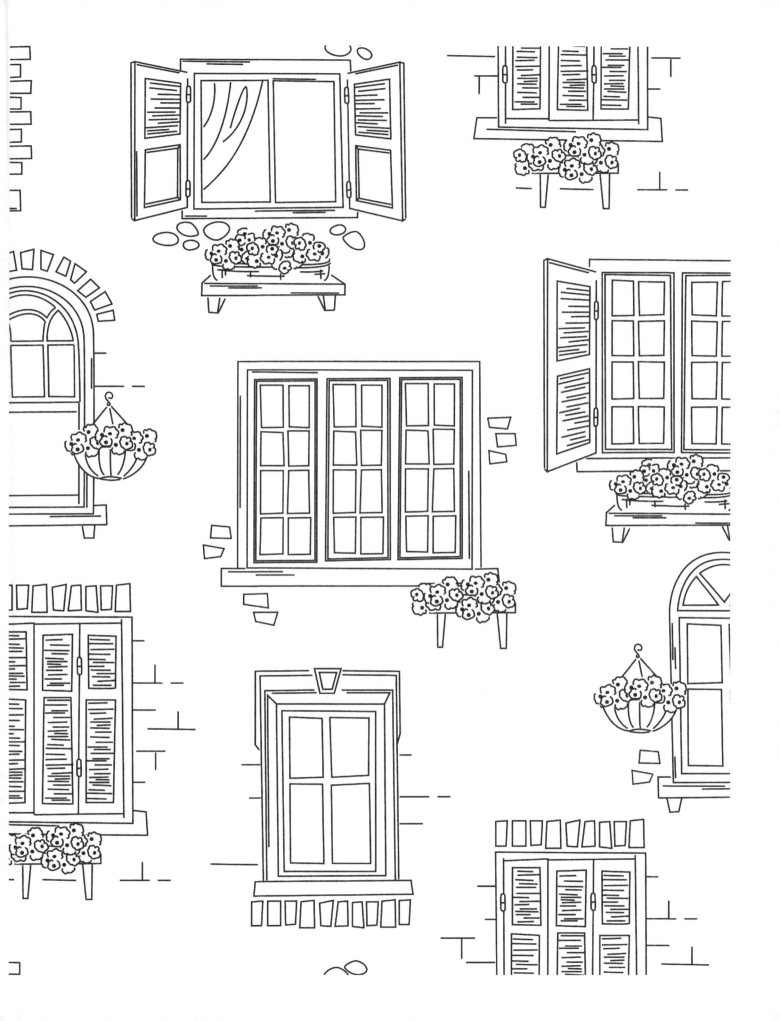

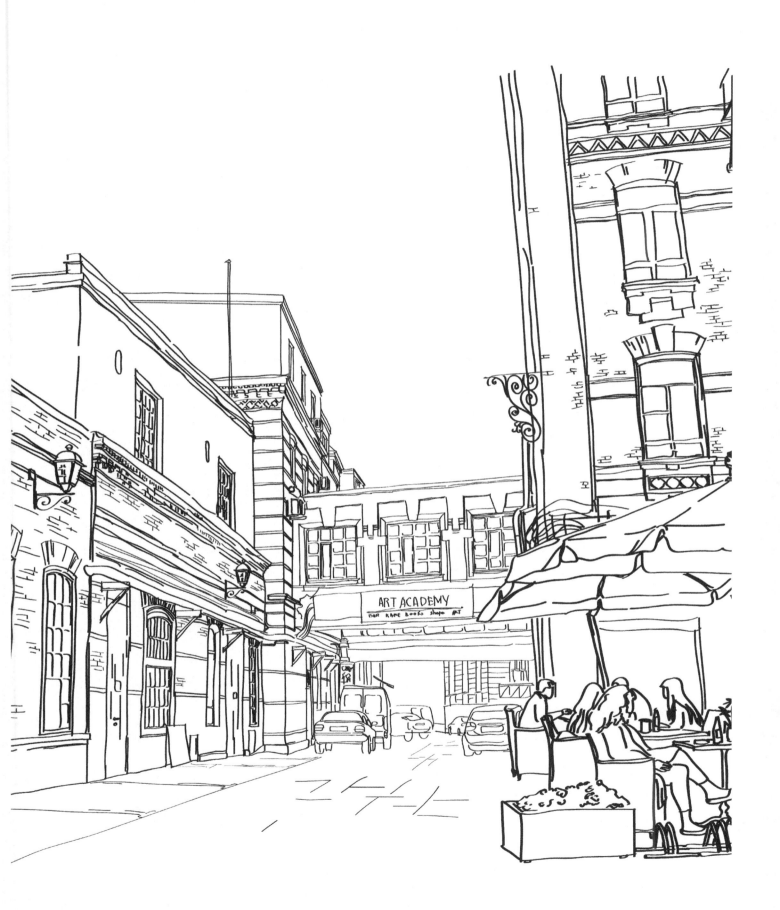

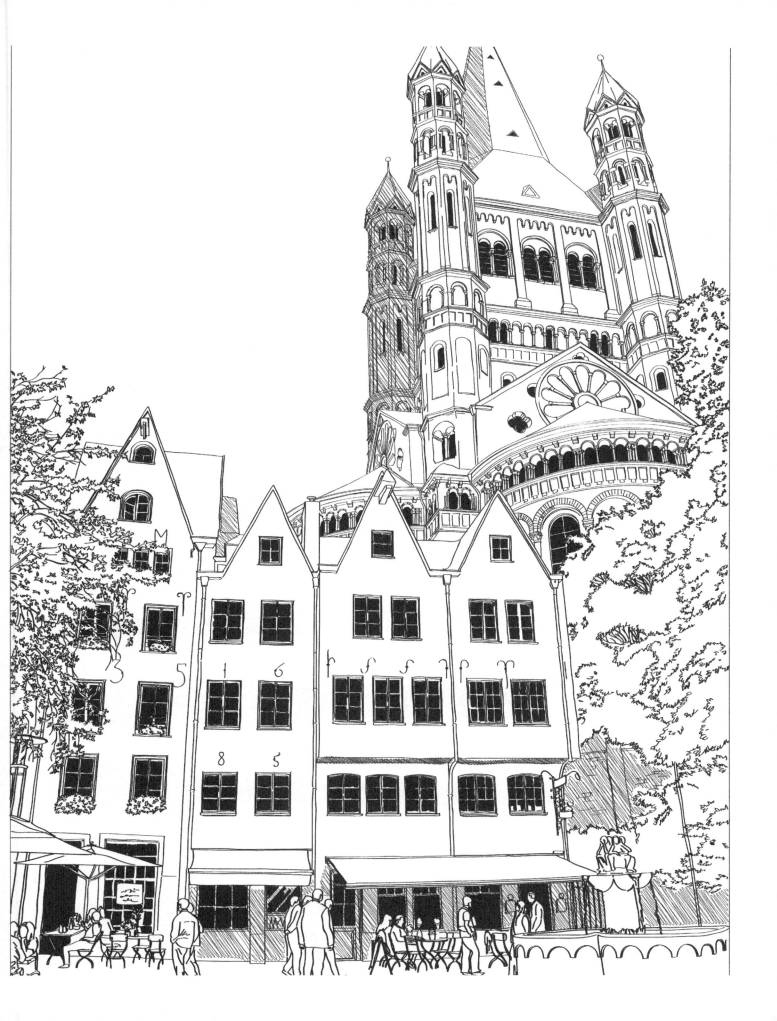

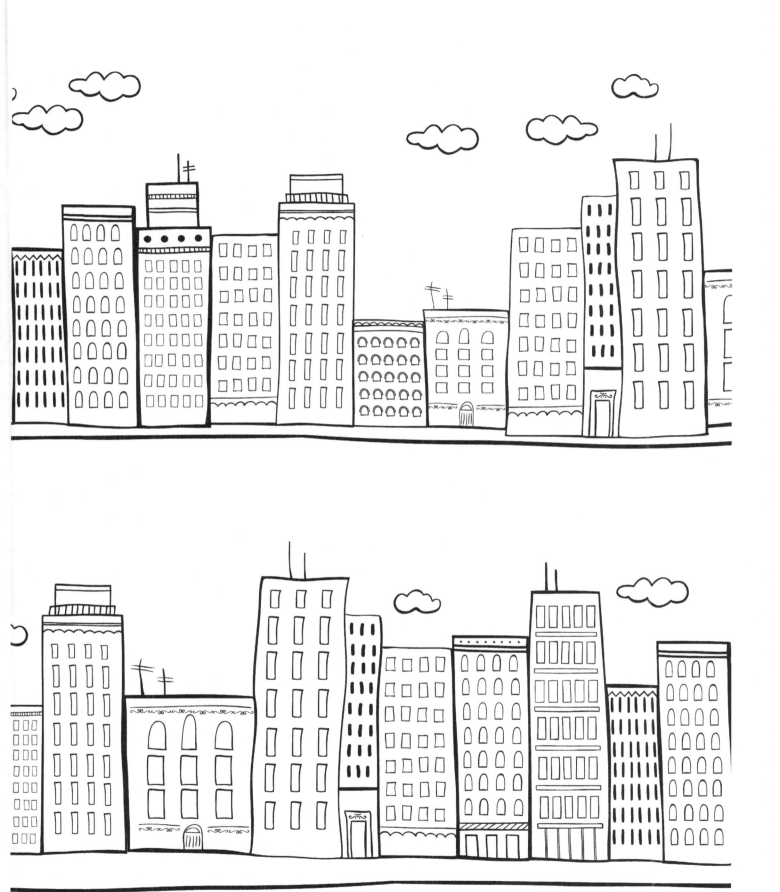

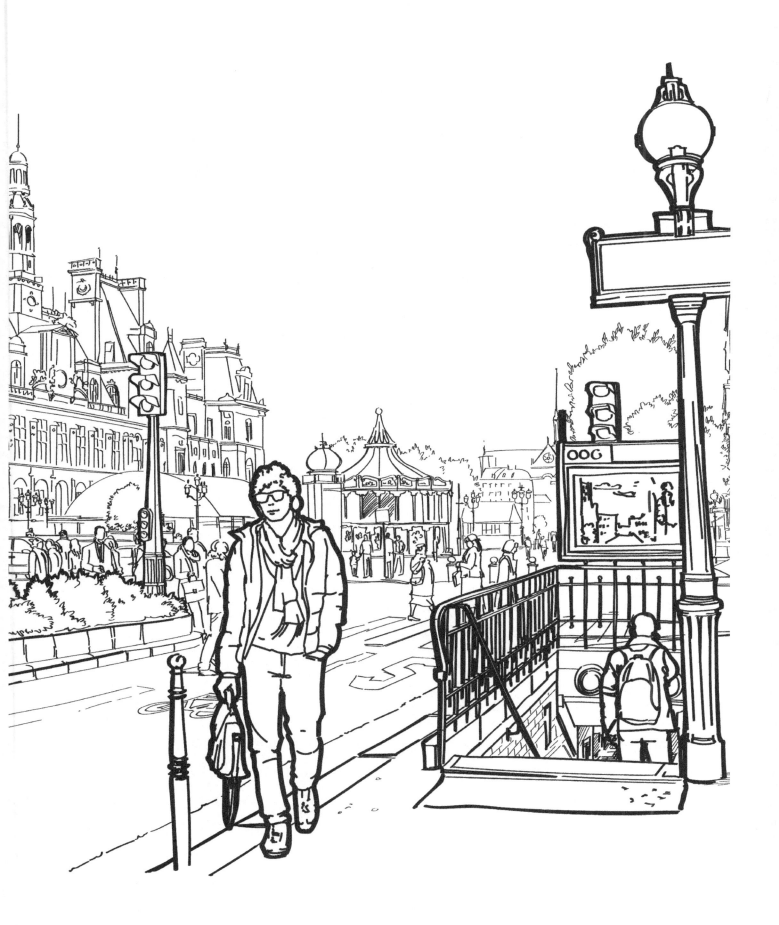

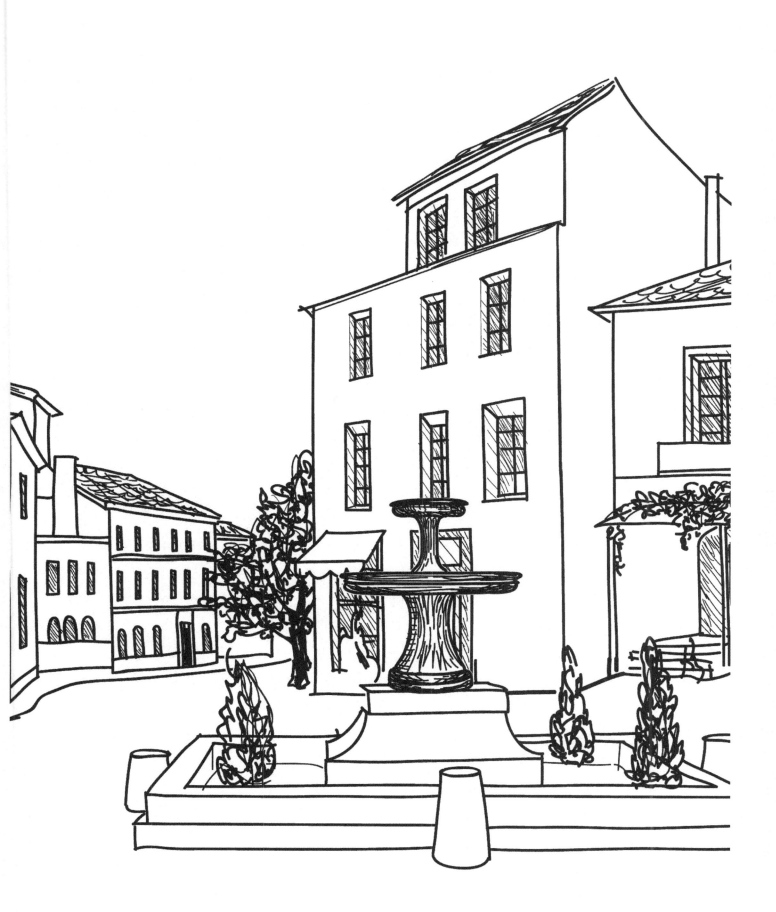

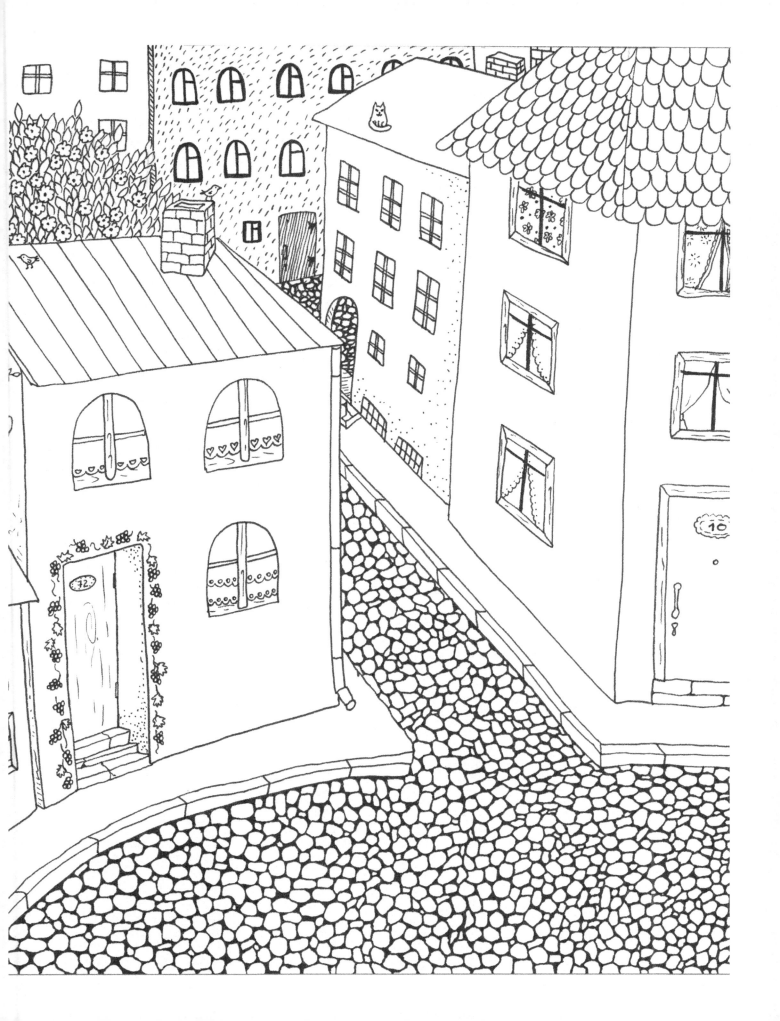

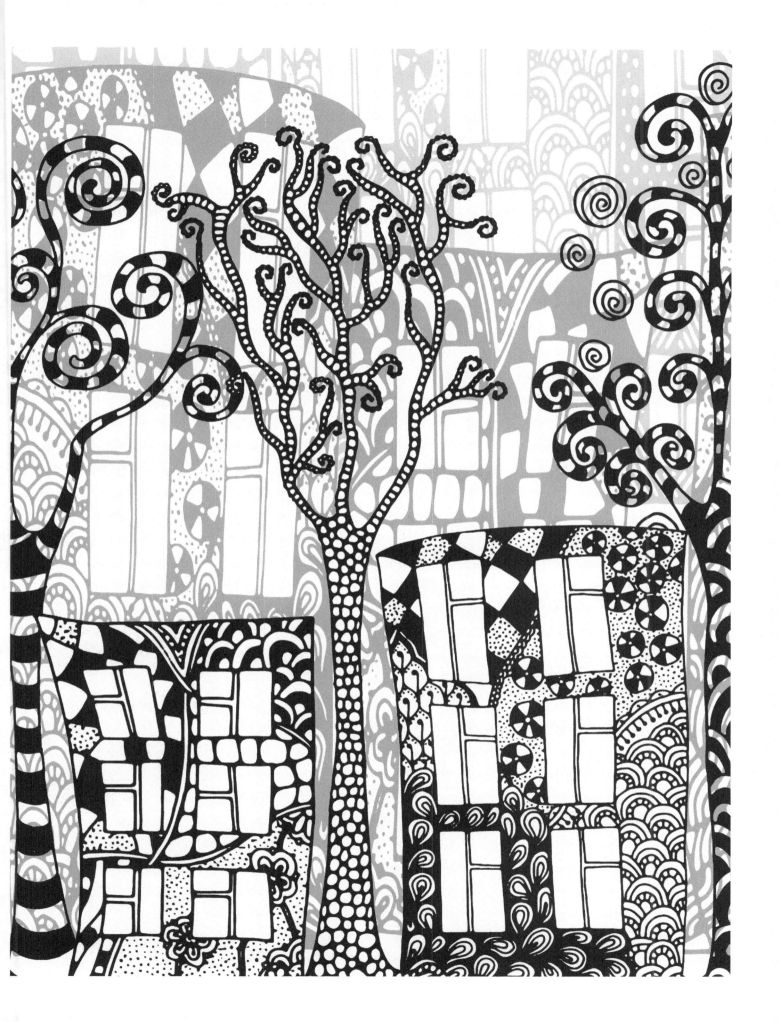

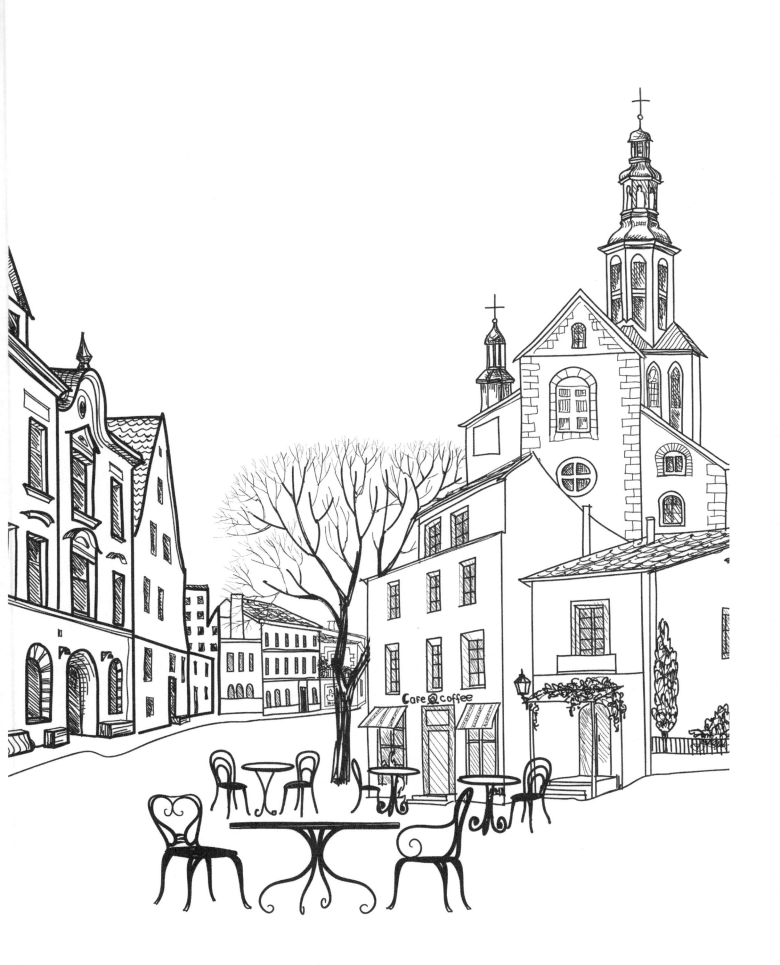

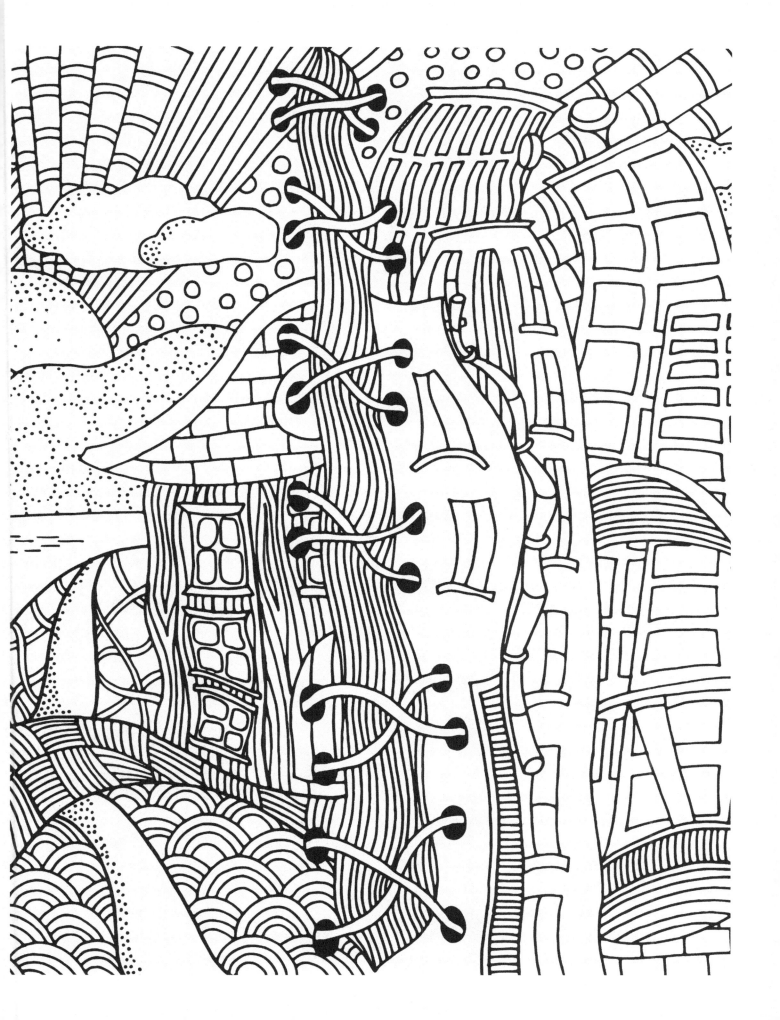

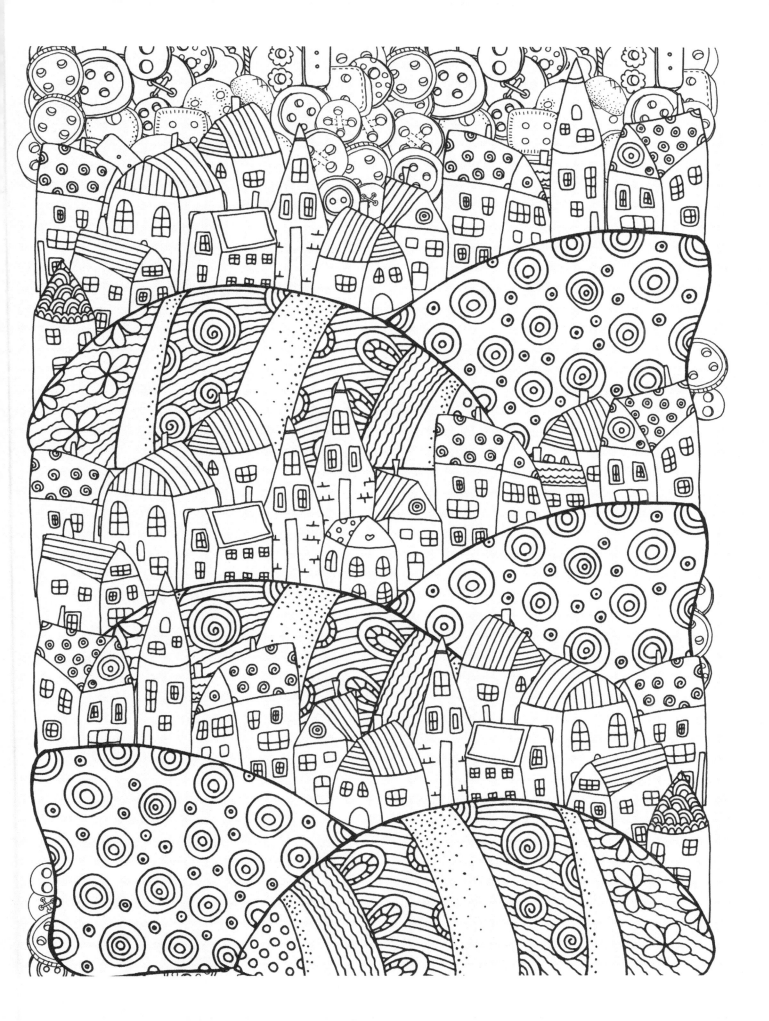

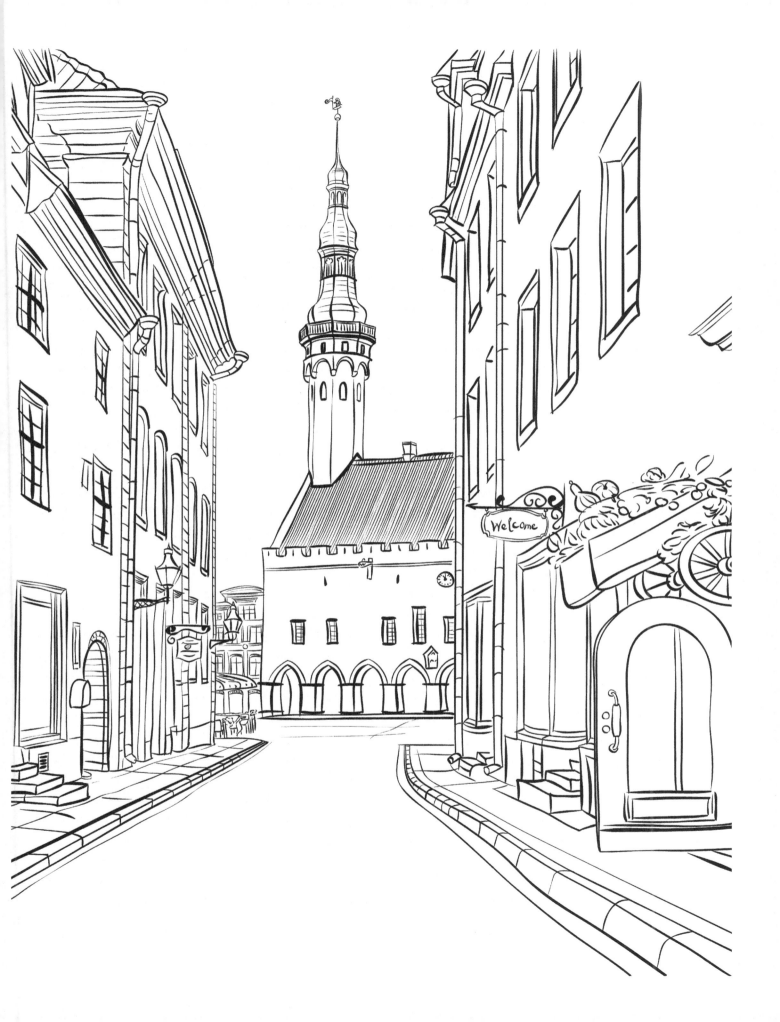

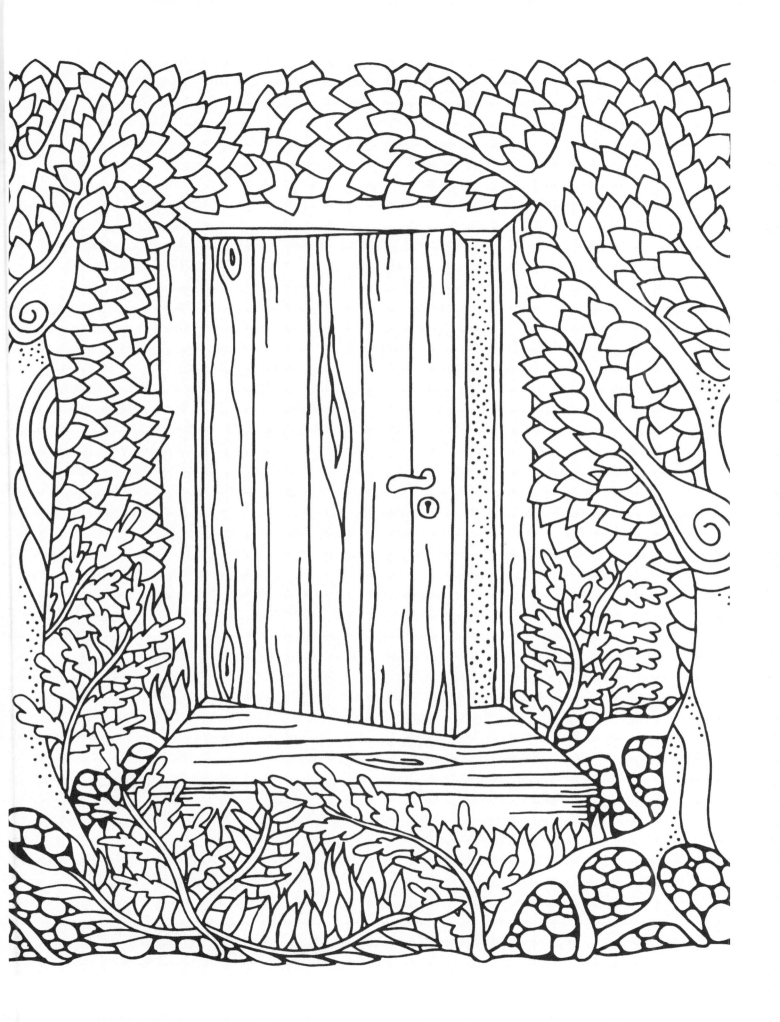

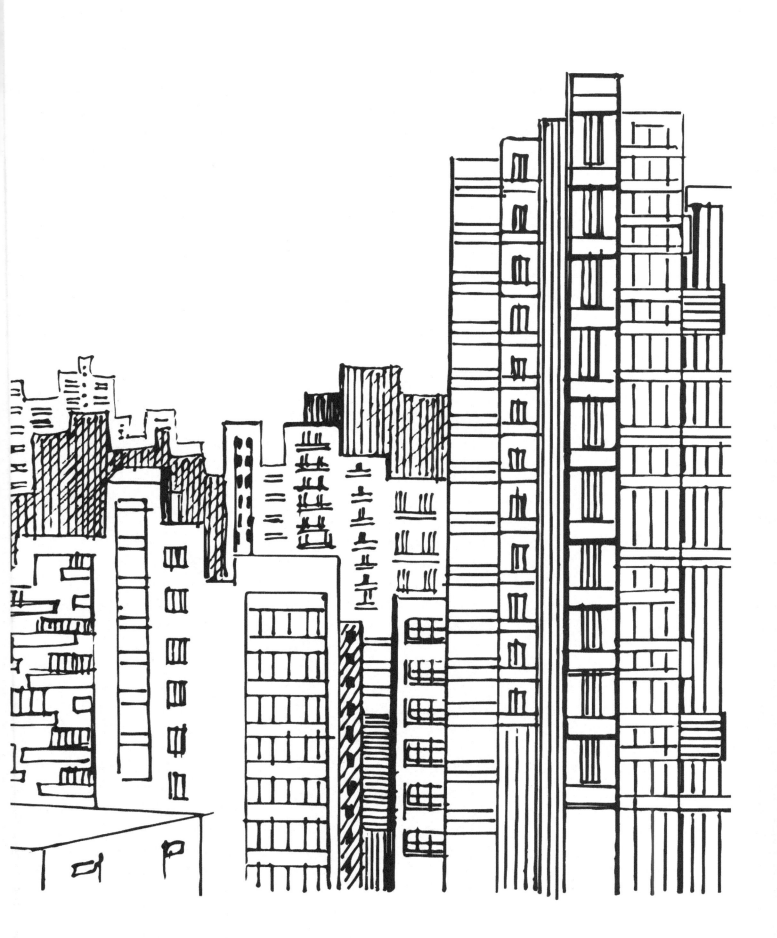

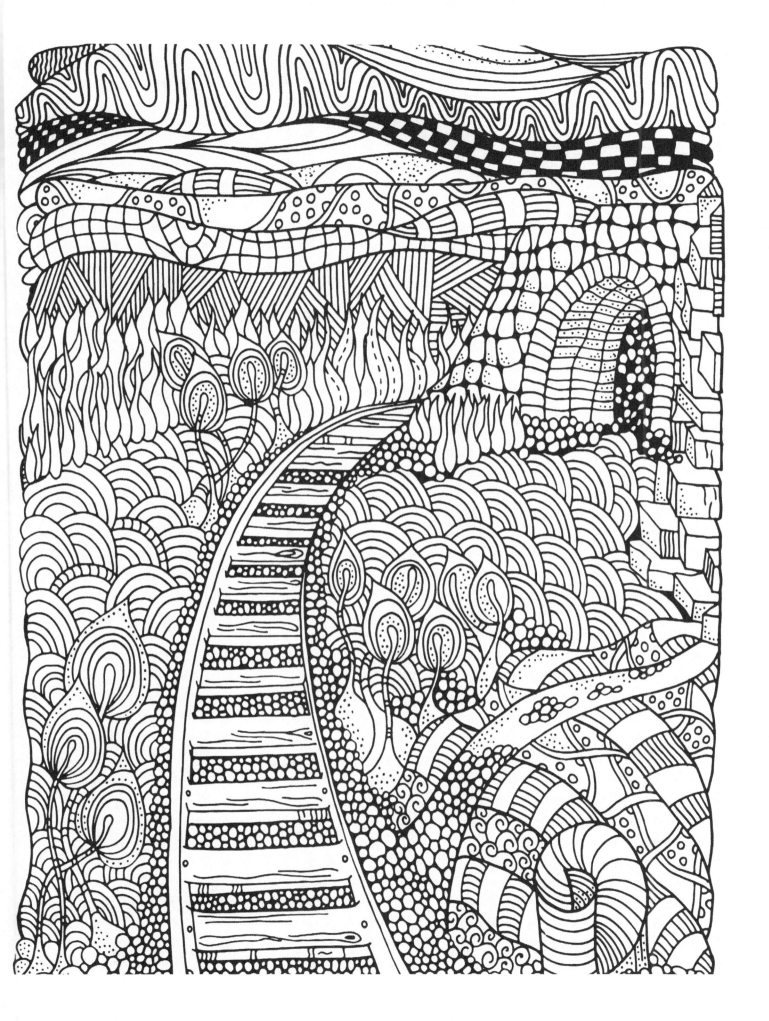

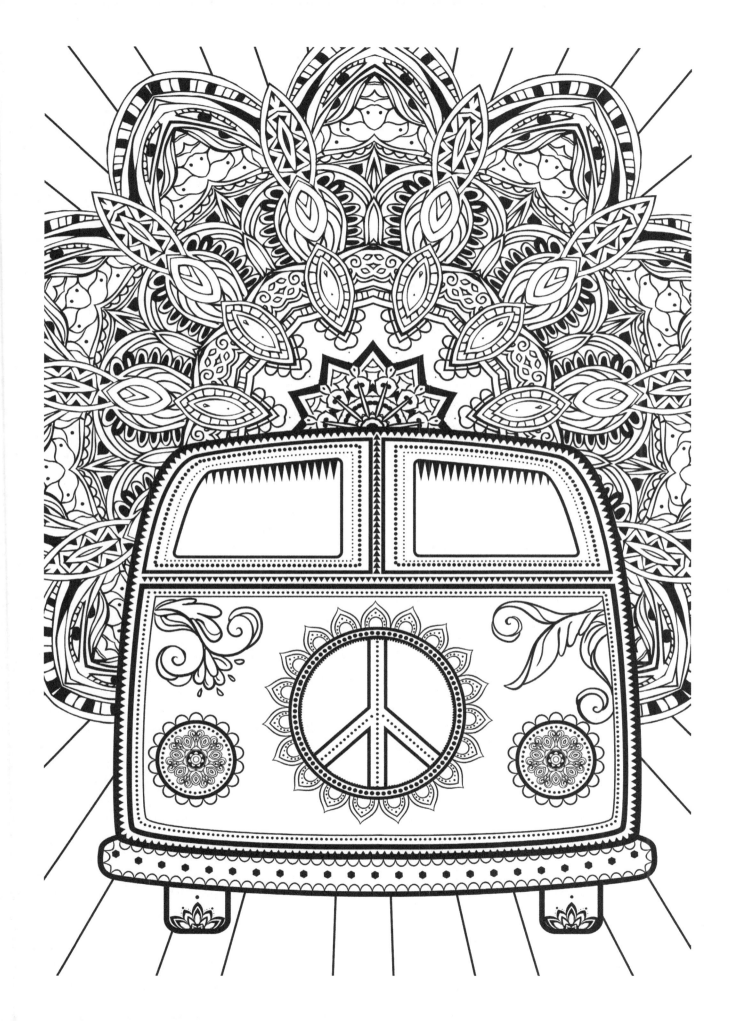

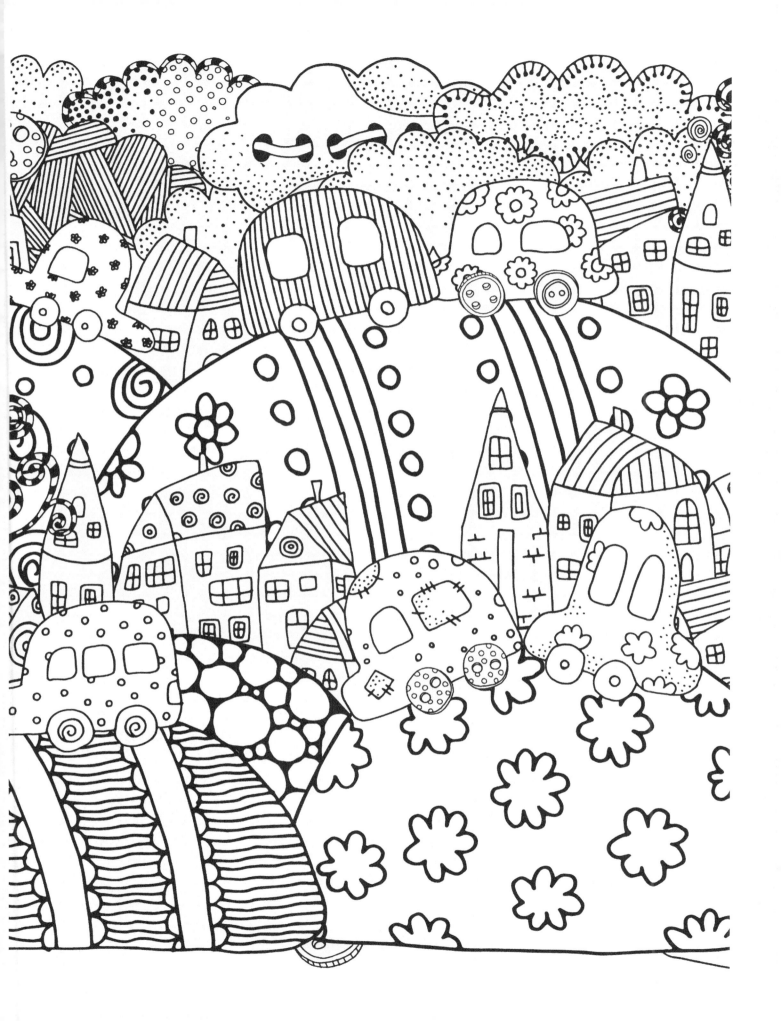

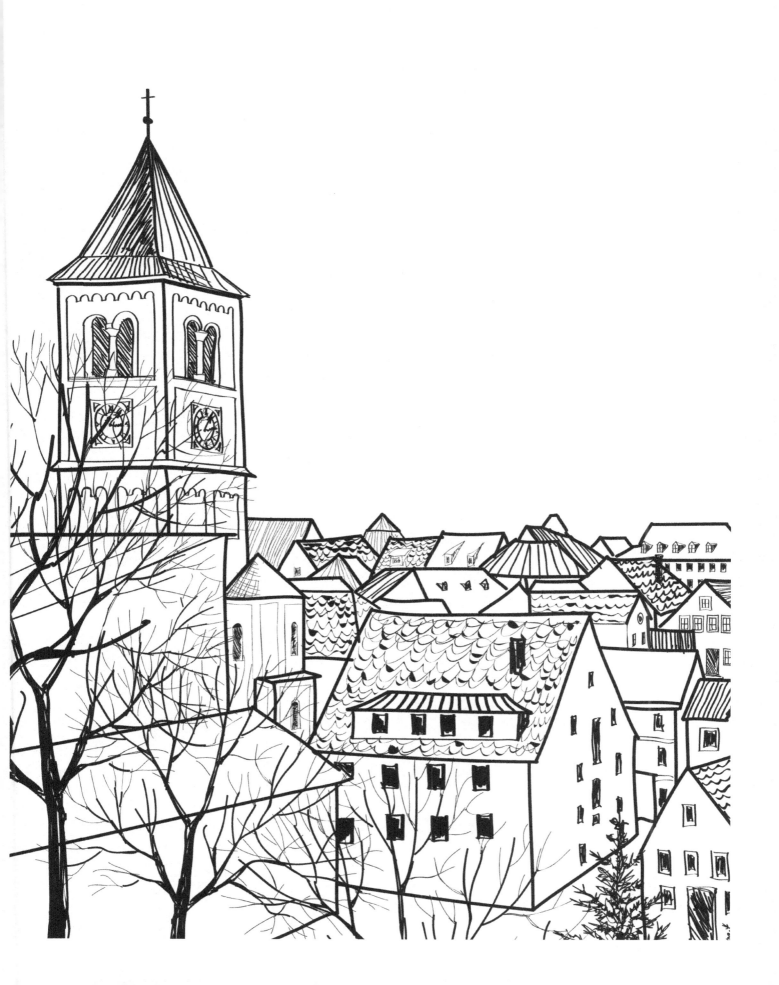

Thank you for purchasing *Colorful Cities: Fun and Fanciful Buildings and Urban Designs.* We hope you enjoy it and that it brings you many hours of coloring pleasure.

Look for other titles in the Coloring Pages for Grown-Ups series:

- *Colorful Butterflies*
- *Colorful Cats*
- *Colorful Owls*